THE Swan FAMILY
HOW THEY CONNECT

T. A. Lunan-Siti

The Swan Family
Copyright © 2020 by T. A. Lunan-Siti

All rights reserved. No part of this publication may be reproduced, distributed, or transmitted in any form or by any means, including photocopying, recording, or other electronic or mechanical methods, without the prior written permission of the author, except in the case of brief quotations embodied in critical reviews and certain other non-commercial uses permitted by copyright law.

Tellwell Talent
www.tellwell.ca

ISBN
978-0-2288-2743-6 (Hardcover)
978-0-2288-2742-9 (Paperback)

Far away up North is a natural habitat for creatures great and small. Where the weather is seasonable with beautiful surroundings of colorful plants and trees; lakes, winding rivers, streams, ponds, waterfalls, marsh, mountain range and a landscape of countless gardens in a natural setting that stimulates the mind.

Among the other water birds that share a large popular pond, lives a bevy of swans along the bank called the Blanc family, and not too far from their nest at the nearby woody pond, is the nest of another bevy known as the Darling family. The swan is the largest member of the fresh water fowl family; they have large webbed feet and long necks sometimes shaped like the letter S. They can glide gracefully on the water and dive for food, but can get quite grumpy on land and hiss when protecting their family of grey or brown baby's called cygnets.

The family of swans were always busy caring for their young and teaching them everything that they needed to know; the Blanc family had a total of seven, dad (cob) and mom (pen) and five little grey cygnets: they stayed close together in the water and on land, always making their calls and sounds to know what to do and where to go. The Darling family had a total of eight, mom (pen) and dad (cob), and six brown cygnets; they are always on the alert and quite busy, as all of the young one's needed to know about everything that was happening around them.

The cygnets were very close to their parents, always trying to follow and do all of the things that their parents did; but sometimes scampered and played about with their friends: at times the Blanc parents would get fussy and call in their babies. Two years went by and the little cygnets grew bigger, taller and all feathered up, they still played together when they could; even though the Blanc family parents were a bit stuck- up and called one of the Darling swans different because he had a red beak and changed from soft brown down, and grew black feathers, while the other swans grew white ones; it did everything they did, ate mostly the same food and there was nothing different about them: the families both lived at the nearby bank of the ponds in their large cozy nest, that was made up of twigs and small branches, bulrush, moss, grass and plant materials; but the black swan was shooed off at times by the Blanc family parents. Cob-cob would go to the lake nearby and frolic, glancing in the water, diving for small fishes, and glide back and forth on the water until the others came to join him; the young swans just thought of the Blanc parent actions as a grown up thing and they were fine: at five years old, they were now grooming their feathers often and they looked quite majestic gliding on the water. When the warm weather came, a certain time of year, all the swans from the far and near regions gather for a summary, this gathering was a very important season for them; it was a time to meet and greet, share tales, ideas and select the most outstanding young swans to compete in games: the winning team for the year got to meet the winners from the games before, and get to form a V shaped wedge in their victory flight.

A very large spot was chosen by the lake and the nearby pond for the events; which included games and prizes, there would be a lot of food, and lots of excitement: the selection for the games were taking place but, some hesitated to pick the Darling's black swan called cob-cob, but as soon as he had passed the test of verifying what swans ate, looked over and was measured, he was qualified by the judges and was selected to compete; the only difference was that cob- cob, had a longer neck and was stouter; none of the other young swans thought that he was different because they all knew him and played together since they were cygnets.

One early morning a little before Sun rise; the whole community of swans were awakened by loud vibrating sounds of honks and wings fluttering over their heads, as the teams and other swans from the far off regions positioned themselves and landed in the lake and on the grounds of the nearby lake and ponds. This was a signal for all the local bevy to get ready and join in with the others that were already at the spot for the games: the location was divided into three parts; one spot for the teams and others that were directly involved in the games, another large spot for the audience of families and on lookers; and one area along the lake that connected to one of the nearby pond was sectioned off with twigs and moss as a spot to be used in the games. On a bright sunny day with clear skies, the games began; home lakes and ponds played against the far away lakes and ponds, both the Blanc and the Darling families were chosen to play for the home team.

The far off lakes and ponds were leading in scores and the home lakes and ponds team started to get tired; the Darling swans noticed that their cob -cob was left out of most of the games, so they asked to give cob -cob, a chance to play more and so they did. The game was 3 to 5 with the far off team leading and there were only 4 games left to play; to swim with only one leg, carry an object on its back across to the woody pond and back to the lake, dive for three things in its beak with one dive, and pick berries from a nearby berry bush while on the lake. The young black swan entered to compete with his feathers raised in an alert display, then positioned himself with the others: when the starter whistle echoed for the one legged swim, he propelled vigorously across to the pond and back in a flash, with one of his webbed feet tucked under his wing, he won.

Then he carried a large piece of root on his back without effort and kept it in place while swimming back and forth from the pond to the lake.

Next, cob -cob, dived into the lake and after a very short time came up with, algae, a small fish, and a frog locked into his sharp edged bill; then the whole crowded area of swans cheered him on.

For the last feat of the game, the black swan stretched out his long S shaped neck while on the lake, and picked a bunch of berries from the nearby bushes.

Then all the different bevy of swans celebrated and honored the winning team with hiss, honks, and grunts; and as the teams winner cob -cob, got many prizes, made a lot of pen, and cob, friends; then the team got chosen to be in a wedge with swans that were winners before them, this made their parents and the whole community of swans very proud. The new winners often flew in a V shape to show their victory win.

The communities of swans far and near had their own nest and bevy's, but they lived in solidarity and supported each other in their endeavors.

The small brown cygnet was adopted by the Darling cob, and pen family, after his family was attacked; they all loved and cared for him as their own. The black swan's first family came from a place called Australia, and even though his beak was red and the Darlings were black it did not matter because they all did the same things and were fine.

Questions and Answers to -Quiz:

Q. What are male swans called? A. (cob)
Q. What are baby swans called? A. (cygnets)
Q. What are female swans called? A. (pen)
Q. What color are baby swans? A. (grey or brown)
Q. What is a group of swans called? A. (a bevy)
Q. What color is a black swan's beak? A. (red)
Q. What do swans do in water? A. (glides and swims gracefully and dives for food)
Q. Name some things that swans will do on land? A. (care for each other and will hiss to protect their babies)
Q. The swan is the: a. smallest b. fattest c. largest of the water fowl family. A. (c)
Q. What are swans called in flight? A. (Wedge)
Q. What color are swans? A. (black, white or black and white)
Q. What sounds do swans make? A. (hiss, honks, grunts,)
Q. What color are their beaks? A. (white swans have red beaks, black swans have red beaks, and the black neck swan has grey beaks with red)
Q. What are some of the things that the swans use to build their nest? A. (twigs, small branches, bulrush, moss, grass, plant materials)
Q. what kind of covering do cygnets have before they grow feathers? A. (Soft down)

Written By: T.A. Lunan-Siti

www.ingramcontent.com/pod-product-compliance
Lightning Source LLC
LaVergne TN
LVHW072016060526
838200LV00059B/4688